Creatures of the Forest Habitat

Opossums

Ada Quinlivan

PowerKiDS press
New York

Published in 2017 by The Rosen Publishing Group, Inc.
29 East 21st Street, New York, NY 10010

First Edition

Editor: Caitie McAneney
Book Design: Mickey Harmon

Photo Credits: Cover (series logo) iLoveCoffeeDesign/Shutterstock.com; cover, pp. 1, 3, 4, 6, 8, 10, 12, 14, 16, 18, 20, 22–24 (background) BlueRingMedia/Shutterstock.com; cover (opossum) Quadxeon/Shutterstock.com; p. 5 (inset) https://upload.wikimedia.org/wikipedia/commons/2/22/Trichosurus_vulpecula_1.jpg; p. 5 (main) Jay Ondreicka/Shutterstock.com; pp. 7, 22 Ronsmith/Shutterstock.com; pp. 9, 21 Steve & Dave Maslowski/Getty Images; p. 10 Joel Sartore/Getty Images; p. 11 Becky Sheridan/Shutterstock.com; p. 13 Karl Maslowski/Getty Images; p. 15 Andrew Skolnick/Shutterstock.com; p. 16 (snakes) komkrit Preechachanwate/Shutterstock.com; p. 16 (birds) Dikky Oesin/Shutterstock.com; p. 16 (mice) Rudmer Zwerver/Shutterstock.com; p. 17 Natalia Kuzmina/Shutterstock.com; p. 19 Tony Campbell/Shutterstock.com.

Cataloging-in-Publication Data

Names: Quinlivan, Ada.
Title: Opossums / Ada Quinlivan.
Description: New York : PowerKids Press, 2017. | Series: Creatures of the forest habitat | Includes index.
Identifiers: ISBN 9781508152682 (pbk.) | ISBN 9781499429282 (library bound) | ISBN 9781499427141 (6 pack)
Subjects: LCSH: Opossums–Juvenile literature.
Classification: LCC QL737.M34 Q85 2017 | DDC 599.2'76–dc23

Manufactured in the United States of America

CPSIA Compliance Information: Batch #BW17PK: For Further Information contact Rosen Publishing, New York, New York at 1-800-237-9932

Contents

America's Marsupial

Marsupials are members of a **mammal** group in which the female carries her babies in a pouch on her belly. One of the most famous marsupials is the kangaroo. You may think that Australia is the only place in the world with marsupials. Did you know that North America is also home to a marsupial? It's called the opossum!

Opossums will eat almost anything. They love to live in forest habitats, as well as neighborhoods. You may see an opossum in your own backyard!

Forest Friend Facts

Many people call "opossums" just "possums." Australian possums are completely different animals though.

This baby opossum is using its great grip to hang onto a branch.

Where in the World?

If you're looking for an opossum, you should know what its range is. An animal's range is where it lives. There are more than 60 **species** of opossum, and each one has its own range.

Some opossum species are found in South America and Central America. The Virginia opossum lives across the eastern and central United States and as far north as southern Canada. This opossum species is also found in the Pacific Northwest **region** of the United States and Canada.

Forest Friend Facts

Opossums are considered an **invasive species** in some places, such as British Columbia and California.

The Virginia opossum is sometimes called the common opossum. This book will focus on the Virginia opossum.

Opossums at Home

An animal's natural home is called its habitat. Opossums make themselves at home nearly everywhere they go. That's because they are very adaptable, or able to change to fit their surroundings. They can live wherever there's enough food shelter, and water.

Forests are great habitats for opossums. Opossums love to spend most of their time in trees. They're very good at climbing, and they sometimes make their nests in holes found in trees.

Forest Friend Facts

Opossums like to live near water. They often make their home near swamps or streams.

Opossums make their way into neighborhoods when there's trash out. They don't mind eating trash!

Built for the Trees

What do opossums look like? They have a pointed **snout** and a skinny tail. They're about the size of a small cat. Female opossums have a pouch, but males don't.

Opossums have bodies that are built for moving in trees. Like some monkey species, opossums have prehensile tails. That means their tails can grasp and hold objects. Opossums can also grasp branches with their sharp claws. Their back feet have **opposable** thumbs, so they can also hold on with their feet.

Forest Friend Facts

Some kinds of porcupines also have prehensile tails. Among them is the well-named prehensile-tailed porcupine.

An opossum has 50 teeth. That's more than any other mammal in North America!

Opossum Babies

Opossum mothers can have up to 20 babies at a time. However, many of them die. Opossum babies are only the size of a honeybee when they're born. They're helpless without their mother.

Opossum babies have to crawl through their mother's fur and into her pouch. The pouch keeps them warm and safe. Baby opossums drink milk inside their mother's pouch. Young opossums can climb in and out of the pouch when they're a little bit older.

Forest Friend Facts

A group of opossums is called a passel.

When opossums are big enough, they can catch a ride on their mother's back!

Playing Possum

"Playing possum" is a way of saying "playing dead." The saying comes from the opossum's great **defense**.

When an opossum feels **threatened** by a predator, it will roll on to its back or side. It makes its body completely stiff. Some opossums close their eyes and some look ahead blankly. This makes the predator think the opossum is already dead. The predator may go away, and then the opossum is free to come back to life!

Some opossums will even stick their tongue out of the side of their mouth to look dead.

Opossums Aren't Picky

Opossums eat both meat and plants, which makes them omnivores. They're also scavengers, which means they will eat dead plants and carrion. Carrion is the dead and rotting bodies of other animals. Opossums also don't mind digging through people's trash to find food.

Opossums will also eat fruit, nuts, and certain grasses. They will eat tiny animals, such as bugs and worms. Sometimes, they hunt mice, birds, and snakes.

mice

birds

snakes

Opossums are most active at night, which makes them nocturnal. If you find that something has been in your trash can at night, it may have been an opossum.

Opossums and People

Opossums are common near communities of people. What should you do if you see one?

Sometimes opossums look scary. If you find one, it might show its many teeth and hiss at you. Even so, opossums are usually not **aggressive**. They're just trying to scare you off, and they'll probably act dead if you get any closer. However, it's still best to leave opossums alone. It's rare, but they may carry **rabies**.

Forest Friend Facts

Sometimes, people eat opossum meat, especially in the southern United States.

Opossums are masters at pretending to be aggressive, even when they're not.

Opossums as Pests

Opossums are often seen as pests, or unwanted and sometimes harmful animals. Sometimes people don't like that they look like rats. Some people are scared when they find opossums in garages and under decks. Farmers sometimes blame opossums for eating their chickens.

Opossums often get a bad **reputation** because they're often found near tipped-over trash cans. However, they're usually just cleaning up the mess made by a larger animal, such as a dog or raccoon.

Forest Friend Facts

Opossums can actually be helpful to you, especially if you have a garden. They eat smaller pests, such as slugs, bugs, and **rodents.**

Opossums move into neighborhoods for food and shelter. If you keep your trash locked up and pet food inside, they might leave your backyard alone.

Forests Forever

People kill opossums for their meat and their fur. Some people kill them because they're considered pests. Other animals, such as bobcats, coyotes, wolves, and owls, also kill opossums. Are opossums at risk of dying out? Luckily this forest creature is very common and isn't in trouble. That's because it's so adaptable to new areas.

Many opossums still rely on forest habitats. When forests are cut down for farms and buildings, opossums are forced into neighborhoods and cities. It's important to keep forests safe for opossums.

Glossary

aggressive: Showing a readiness to attack.

defense: A feature of a living thing that helps keep it safe.

invasive species: Plants or animals from one area that spread quickly in a new area and harm native plants and animals.

mammal: A warm-blooded animal that has a backbone and hair, breathes air, and feeds milk to its young.

opposable: Able to be placed against one or more of the fingers or toes on the same hand or foot such as the human thumb.

rabies: A deadly disease that affects the central nervous system. It is carried in the spit of some animals.

region: A large area of land that has a number of features in common.

reputation: The views that are held about something or someone.

rodent: A small, furry animal with large front teeth, such as a mouse or rat.

snout: An animal's nose and mouth.

species: A group of plants or animals that are all the same kind.

threatened: Likely to be harmed.

Index

Websites

Due to the changing nature of Internet links, PowerKids Press has developed an online list of websites related to the subject of this book. This site is updated regularly. Please use this link to access the list: www.powerkidslinks.com/forest/opos